And if you read well, you will not sin against the Lord.

2nd Enoch[i]

THE EGYPTIAN ORIGIN OF CHRISTIANITY

Edited by
Lisa Ann Bargeman

© Copyright 2002 Lisa Ann Bargeman. All rights reserved.

No part of this publication may be reproduced, stored in a retrieval system, or transmitted, in any form or by any means, electronic, mechanical, photocopying, recording, or otherwise, without the written prior permission of the author.

Front cover image from *The Ancient Egyptian Book of the Dead*, trans. by R.O. Faulkner, ed. by Carol Andrews, copyright 1972, rev. ed. 1985; by permission of the University of Texas Press and The British Museum Press; p. 183.

National Library of Canada Cataloguing in Publication

Bargeman, Lisa Ann, 1974-
     The Egyptian origin of Christianity / Lisa Ann Bargeman.
Includes bibliographical references.
ISBN 1-55369-505-4
     1. Christianity--Origin. 2. Egypt--Religion--Influence.
I. Title.
BR129.B37 2002   270.1   C2002-901996-6

Printed in Victoria, Canada

TRAFFORD

This book was published *on-demand* in cooperation with Trafford Publishing.
On-demand publishing is a unique process and service of making a book available for retail sale to the public taking advantage of on-demand manufacturing and Internet marketing. **On-demand publishing** includes promotions, retail sales, manufacturing, order fulfilment, accounting and collecting royalties on behalf of the author.

Suite 6E, 2333 Government St., Victoria, B.C. V8T 4P4, CANADA
Phone   250-383-6864   Toll-free   1-888-232-4444 (Canada & US)
Fax   250-383-6804   E-mail   sales@trafford.com
Web site   www.trafford.com   TRAFFORD PUBLISHING IS A DIVISION OF TRAFFORD HOLDINGS LTD.
Trafford Catalogue #02-0318   www.trafford.com/robots/02-0318.html

10   9   8   7   6

CONTENTS

Dedication		6
About the Author		7
Acknowledgments		7
Introduction		11
PART I	**CEREMONY**	
	Rites	15
	Trinities	19
PART II	**SACRED LANGUAGE**	
	The Origin of the Texts	23
	Lexicon	27
	Personification	32
	Motifs	34
PART III	**DISSEMINATION**	
	The Egyptian Mystery System	41
	Maat	49
PART IV	**REDEMPTION**	
	The Jesus/Osiris Connection	54
	The Mary/Isis Connection	56
PART V	**IMPORTANCE OF THE EIGHTEENTH DYNASTY**	
	Akhenaten	61
	Nefertiti	66
PART VI	**CONSEQUENCES**	
	Roles of Women	70
	Religious Censorship	71
PART VII	**TALL TALES**	
	Genesis	75
	The Great Flood	80
PART IIX	**GENERAL PRACTICES**	
	The Seven Sacraments	83
	Angels	89
	The Gates of Saint Peter	90
Conclusion		91
Bibliography		93
Endnotes		96

DEDICATION

For my Mother, Jaye, and David

Acknowledgments

I would like to thank all of my family and friends who encouraged me to write this book and to pursue my goals.
Thank you!

8

Who can say whether Egyptian mummies may not have had something to do with the Christian concept of "resurrection of the flesh", which belongs neither to the Old Testament religion nor to that of the Greeks.... Other religions, such as those of the Israelites and of the ancient Greeks, teach that God's power does not extend beyond the limits of this earthly existence: it cannot penetrate the dark realms of Sheol or the gates of Hades. This makes the Egyptian phenomena all the more important and specific.... [Their] sacred act[s]... entitle us to exempt the Egyptians from the charges hurled at them by Old Testament writers for pagan idol worship, which the Israelites themselves often copied.... It is... doubtful whether [Judaism] could gain so much influence as Egypt did upon the nascent Christian religion....[ii]

INTRODUCTION

    Perhaps with the publication of this book it can finally be regarded as fact that Egypt's influence on modern theology is most strongly perceived through Christian beliefs and practices. I will primarily be focusing here on the direct ceremonial parallels between the modern Roman Catholic Church and ancient Egyptian ceremony. In both systems, there is a great pride in tradition and the detailed specificity with which rituals are carried out. While all forms of Christianity display strong parallels to the rituals of ancient Egypt, perhaps the strongest examples can be seen in Roman Catholicism.

    It might be said that it is impossible to compare ancient Egyptian practice with a religion which occurred much later and which on the surface appears to be entirely different. However, the case may be made that, like a staircase, each evolutionary step builds upon the one before it. Literary and historical evidence of the route can be directly traced to ancient Egypt.

    Generally around 2250 B.C.E. invaders came through the English Channel "from Libya, by way of Spain, Southern and Northern France, or by way of Spain, Portugal and Brittany...."[iii]

"At different periods in the second millenium B.C.E., a confederacy of mercantile tribes, called in Egypt 'the people of the sea,' were displaced from the Aegean area by invaders from the northeast and southeast; that some of these wandered north, along already established trade routes, and eventually reached Britain and Ireland; and that others wandered west, also along established trade routes, some elements reaching Ireland by way of West Africa and Spain. Still others invaded

Syria and Canaan, among them the Philistines, who captured the shrine of Hebron in southern Judea [and took it from] the Edomite clan of Caleb, but the Calebites, ...allies of the Israelite tribe of Judah, recovered it about two hundred years later and took over a great part of the Philistine religion at the same time."[iv]

Ancient travelers'were widely dispersed from North Africa, where all evolutionary theorists agree that human life began, carrying with them their traditions and customs. Therefore, religious hermeneutics can only be properly achieved through acknowledgment of the source material. The incantations from The Book of the Dead, for example, began circa three thousand B.C.E., much earlier than any Biblical works; yet The Bible is seen as the seat of all morality.

The importance of the Egyptian sway can no longer be denied. Siegfried Morenz, Director of the University of Liepzig Institute of Egyptology, remarked that "the influence of the Egyptian religion on posterity is mainly felt through Christianity and its antecedents. Egypt's contribution to the Old Testament is acutally a product of that country's relationship with Syria; its contribution to the New Testament, indeed, even to early Christian theology, must be seen as a special instance of that general influence exerted by Egypt upon the Hellenistic world." It is that influence which will be explored herein in terms of modern day practices of particularly the Roman Catholic Church in order that the true nature of religion as a whole may be elucidated.

I CEREMONY

14

RITES

Imagine, if you will, opening the doors to a shrine, and blessing yourself with holy water as you enter. You prepare to sit and pray, for God can provide solace from all earthly problems. Once you have confided in statues (imbued with the spirit of the living God) and sung the hymn, others join you in the chant with relics and devotional items. Litanies are read. A priest gives the sermon, makes the Sign of the Peace, and prepares the celebrants for communion. The morning hymn in an Egyptian church was: Awake graciously, which meant in peace; thou awakest graciously, so let us awaken graciously in peace.[v]

These are Egyptian rites, and it is tradition rather than coincidence that have made them so. Astoundingly, these rituals have been flawlessly perpetuated for five thousand years. But even more astounding is the fact that this miracle has gone for the most part unrecognized.

Papal custom rejects change. Modern governments have been much more amendment-worthy than papal law through time. But rigidity has its benefits, for it has successfully preserved such theological solemnity from before the third and fourth centuries B.C.E. to the present.

Nowhere can this be better demonstrated than through the mass service.

> The priest opens the shrine containing the image, prostrates himself before it, cleanses and perfumes it with incense, adorns and embellishes it, places crowns upon it, anoints it and beautifies it with cosmetic. Finally he wipes away his prints."[vi]

This sounds like the Roman Catholic tabernacle rather than an ancient Egyptian rite, and indeed, these customs can be compared to the daily cleansing of the monstrance and cup, as well as that of daily elaborate adornment.

The tabernacle which houses the monstrance and cup is a version of another Middle Eastern relic, the Judaic Ark of the Covenant. The Most-Holy-of-Holies contained therein is preserved in the sanctity of darkness. "The Egyptian gods would have shared Yahveh's wish 'that he would dwell in thick darkness' (I Kings viii, 12)." This is also true of the Indian Bhagavadgita, for "at midnight, in the thickest darkness, the Dweller in every heart revealed Himself in the divine."[vii]

Egyptian *serdab* statues were locked away behind closed doors and kept in barely-illumined rooms. Seen only by gazing through peepholes provided for the purpose, clergy were permitted the privilege of gazing upon the dark storehouses of sacred items.

Today the Ark of the Covenant is not usually moved from the sanctum of the church, but traditionally the Egyptian Ark was quite mobile. Both priests and statuary were floated in symbolic barks across the water — the "communion" came to everybody. Local Christian festivals of the saints, such the San Janiero annual festival in New York city, parallel those of the ancient gods.

The true meaning of praise through communion is the unification of multifarious peoples to god through the use of a symbolic or sacred food. Communion is not a new idea; Hatshepsut wrote of Amon, he "is my bread and I drink from its dew. I am of one body with him."[viii] Hatshepsut, who ruled for eighteen years before dying circa 1468 B.C.E., wrote these words well over one thousand years before the life of Jesus Christ, circa 4 B.C.E. to 29 C.E.

(Meals could also be used as commemorative memorials. Provisions after Egyptian burial rites were much like our protocol for funeral repasts. The notion of prayer offering is thus classical not only in burial rites, at home, and in temple but also at a wall or gate. With reference to the "Wailing Wall" in Israel, this theme occurs in Egyptian lamentations and reflects the selfsame desire to bring supplications to a structure, be it church, temple, headstone, or other, in order to ensure their divine honor.)[ix]

As communion invokes fasting, a devout Roman Catholic fasts for an hour before communion's receipt and consumes particular fish rather than meat on Fridays. Within Roman Catholicism, there appears to be no particular explanation for the fasting. The authoritative Nihil Obstat- and Imprimatur- endorsed Dictionary of the Liturgy states that "this rule is not based on scientific data.... Abstinence from meat is especially recommended.... Canon Law for the world prescribes abstinence on all Fridays (Canon 1251.)"[x] However, of Egyptian derivation are such fasts as those to and from fish, resulting from legend of holy sacrament, where "Osiris... was torn [apart] by Set.... When Isis reassembled the pieces the phallus had disappeared, eaten by a letos-fish. This accounts for the priestly fish-taboo in Egypt, relaxed only one day in the year."[xi] The fish-taboo would have been practiced as a symbolic means of preserving and upholding reverence for the god.

The symbolic communion itself is demonstrated in part through the show of demonstrative attire worn while serving. The basal garment in both Catholic and traditional Egyptian religious societies is the loosely-fitting white vestment or alb, which may be accompanied by other decorative ceremonial attire as needed. Indicative also is the miter, a form of the ancient "triple crown." The present day Pope wears the triple crown in the form of the large, pointed, symbolic headpiece, as was counterexemplified in Egypt by use of the trinitarious interlaid large, pointed red, white, and blue crowns (interesting choice of colors to Americans); one for North Egypt, one for South, and the third for special unification and representational event symbolism.

Commonly used is the crozier of Biblical tradition as a

shepherd's tool rather than as a weapon. The Egyptian emblems of royalty, the crook and the flail were tools of guidance rather than weapons. They are "tool[s] of soft material comparable to those used... in the eastern Mediterranean to collect laudanum from bushes. The pastoral role of the king is emphasized in certain literary and religious texts in which mankind is seen as the herd of cattle to be tended by the creator and by his issue on earth the king."[xii]

Clearly the most antiquitous origins of the Christian motif were not based on primary source material. The need for a mediator, a son of god, as an all-powerful shepherd and a begotten savior living among the common man, begins to take shape as the driving force.

TRINITIES

If God is essential energy, then god exists as plural and singular at the same time. Each god, as an aspect of the same, can meet the claim that "all gods are three": Father (the stern and wrathful lawgiver), Son (the gentle and kind-hearted sacrificial lamb) and Holy Ghost (the spiritual paraclete). As for "Amon, Re and Ptah... 'Hidden' is his name as Amon, he is Re in face, and his body is Ptah".[xiii] Khnum-Atum/Aten-Re Ptah (Father Gods), Osiris-Horus (Son Gods) and Min/Amen (Holy Spirit Gods) are the Father, Son, and Holy Ghost. In fact, Aten's true name is "Re-Harakhte, rejoicing on the Horizon in the Aspect of the Light which is in the Aten."[xiv] (By the way, it is from this Aten-Amen that we get the word "Amen.")

The linking of the god-names here is essential. All of these gods represent the same basic concepts. They were often combined, if not only in name, then in concept. They are enumerated so that the varied nature of the pantheon may be noted as allowing for both the singularity and the unity of the monotheistic religions.

Upon initially pondering the Christian trinity, it does not seem reasonable for any god to bring himself down to a secondary level, for any reason. Why would a sole supreme force exist as itself as well as it's son, also becoming something not *a priori*, and voluntarily placing itself in the secondary position?

While no reason exists in modern Roman Catholicism, Egyptian literature does provide a reason. God becomes the son when the king, a "personification of the cosmic god, was put out of joint by... Re, who won supremacy and demoted the king to the rank of his son, responsible to him."[xv] The trinity consists of three equals. Plural, dissimilar aspects possess the same essential energy.

Egyptian trinities were conceived in order to elevate the status of a minor deity to that of a major one. Theoretically, any two lower gods could be adjuncted to a more powerful, omnipotent creator in order to reinforce their power.

Catholic trinities are used for the same purpose as the Egyptian. The primary trinity of Jesus, Mary, and Joseph is so powerful that it forms the crux of Roman Catholic thought. It is the inspiration for the largest-scale Christian holiday, and has elevated Mary to virtually the level of God himself.

"The trinity was a major preoccupation of Egyptian theologians, [but] ...we also find such evidence in Greek only one generation before the beginnings of Christian theological speculation...."[xvi] This evidence supports the fact that trinities are just another Egyptian innovation, like racetracks, and mining.

II SACRED LANGUAGE

22

THE ORIGIN OF THE TEXTS

There were, according to George M. James, maxims in ancient times, as now, written on temple walls and above doorway entrances. These became frequently quoted and served as memory aids to remind practitioners of the faith. The resounding cry in European courts of, "eat, drink and be merry, for tomorrow we may die," is a corruption of the Egyptian, "Gaze here," (at a physical symbol of mortality,) "and drink and be merry; for when you die, such will you be."[xvii]

The word and concept of "god" is in itself an Egyptian invention and was written NTR in their language.[xviii] It has been supposed that the substance natron (a natural salt from which soap is made) formed the root, symbolizing purity and renewal.

Jesus' and Osiris' stories, presented as second- and third-party chronicles, were used to support the idea of the pre-destined creator. Since it was the fulfillment of prophecy that these things occurred, written accounts were held sacred, such as *The Bible* and *The Ancient Egyptian Book of the Dead*.

Marxist philosophy maintains that bourgeois will suppress privileged information in order to deem themselves "enlightened." Middle Eastern god-founding nations deemed themselves "the Chosen People" and elected that a sacred language be kept within their territorial boundaries. Arabs, too, opted for such selective classification, which affected the manner in which their languages were written and dispersed. It is an unusual, corresponding fact, for example, that both the Hebrew and the Egyptian languages contain no vowels.

Opposites were more likely to be paralleled in everyday

speech, usage later to be borrowed by Biblical authors. For example, "Seth... is the great Wild Bull, he is the soul of Geb."[i] Explanation: Seth is primarily a negative god (the Christian parallel being Satan.) Geb is a positive god, the god of earth. Here a positive can be used to describe a negative without ruining the reputation of the god. Seth can be properly understood as the wild, raw and untamed desert earth.

Many English words and phrases have been borrowed from the Egyptian. The dictionary lists Egyptian words adapted into English (ka, ankh and ba) but how many more must there be. *The Bible*'s title itself is a nomen of the Syrian city under strong Egyptian influence, Byblos. As a goddess associated with Egypt's celestial cow Hathor, Byblos was famous in her city of "little books" for the papyrus trade. It followed then that Byblos, the title of a Syrian goddess, became the ancient title for our Judaeo-Christian Word of God.[ii] *The Bible* was named for a town goddess whose worship was therein forbidden.

Conversely, the Egyptian god Set, or Seth was identified with Baal, or Baal-Seth, who became the Israelite god known as Baal-zebub or Beelzebub to the cities that took his name. Therefore doubly foreboding is the claim that *The Bible*'s greatest evil, Satan, was the word for God.

Other god-names may also be derived from Egyptian. Tiamat (possibly a corruption of -maat) was identified with the universal mother Akhet also known as Nut and was similarly an aquarian Hittite goddess. Maau, a feline goddess, inspired the cat-call, "meow", and her name became associated with the breed of domestic cat known as the Egyptian Maau to this day.

It is known that many bird species-names are Egyptian in origin, ibis, for example, also affording proof that the Biblical writers used Egyptian nomenclature as reference material. As another avian example, the god Buto may have contributed to the Latin word Buteo referring to the avian hawk-related class, since Buto as a snake god could have been associated with the words "snake-hunter." This is supported by the fact that Buteo allies were significant in ancient Egyptian culture, as is demonstrated by the falcon-god Horus, the vulture goddesses, i.e., Nehkbet, and the class' pervasiveness unto phoenetic characters (the representation for the letter m is an owl, and vowels a,e, and o are represented by a vulture).

Buto's influence could also be felt through items such as the uraeus or snake-like headdress, in that they harnessed and directed the power for heka/heqa (power) through the pharoah. "Heka" referred to the unification of positive and negative forces, the harnessing of which was called magic. The Egyptians who invented the goddesses Heka and Heqet had their idea adopted by the Greeks in the goddess Hecate (harbinger of death and black magic,) while today the English language employs words like "hecatomb" and "hex." The word heka refers to the unification of positive and negative forces, the harnessing of which was called magic.

The subject of language-likening is certainly worthy of further study, and may shed light on the ancient pronunciations of words for which we have limited record of spoken combinations and hermeneutic knowledge. The word "wad" in Egyptian, for example, was used to identify the color green. To this day the word wadi is used to refer to places where greenery and water can be found in the desert during the rainy season. It seems certain that other desert miracles, such as that of the "manna" fed to Biblical travelers, had something to do with Egyptian linguistics; i.e., the word for power being also associated with "mana."[iii]

In order to better study texts, however, scholars should agree on a translation based on one set of original god-names. Uniformity in the field of Egyptology appears to be presently impossible because of previous authors' and translators' incongruent attempts. For example, common Egyptian names are frequently referred to in Greek. This is perhaps another misappropriation of Egyptian credits and therefore for this reason I refer to the Egyptian language-names by the closest available translation (Amenhotep versus Amenophis) as often as possible.

It is no longer possible to do this, however, in all cases, because there are many instances by which the original word has been so translated that it is no longer recognized by its original god-name; i.e., Pai has been forever turned into the Apis bull.

On the following pages I have provided some information which may prove useful in noting changes between our languages. It is a dictionary, if you will, and since the information with which I have worked with indicated vowels, the vowels have also been indicated, although I am unfamiliar with the actual criterion for this practice.[iv]

LEXICON

EGYPTIAN	TRANSLATION
n (prep.)	of
aa (adj.)	mighty
aat (n.)	festival of sacrifice
abw (n.)	purity
ah (v.)	entrap
ah.s (adj.)	useful
ak (n.)	House of Life
am (n.)	devourer
anmw (n.)	falcon idols
api (v.)	to fly (indicated as present tense)
awn (v.)	to covet
biat (adj.)	maternal; virtuous (as in Bast)
bs (n.)	form
bta (adj.)	wrong
bw (n.)	place
d (n.)	mountain
dat (n.)	realm of the dead
dd (conj.)	that's
dha (adj.)	oppressive
Dhwty (n.)	the messenger (title of Thoth)
di (v.)	to give or put
dr (prep.)	from
ds (n.)	himself
dsr (adj.)	hidden; sacred
dt (n.)	command/body/eternity
grg (v.)	to form or to lie/deceive
grw (n.)	silent man
ha (n.)	festival
ha i (adj.)	glad
hai (v.)	to appear/descend, as in a revelation
Hapy (n.)	Nile

EGYPTIAN	TRANSLATION
har (n.)	land
hasti/hati (n.)	foreigner (reminds one of Hatti, and the Hitties)
haswt (n.)	mountains
hhw (n.)	deluge
hi (n.)	overseer
hm (adj.)	ignorant
hm (n.)	tongue (suspiciously similar to the word hum)
hm (n.)	sanctuary magistrates
hmhmt (n.)	fame
hmnw (n.)	the Ogdoad
hmww (n.)	artisan
hni (v.)	settles
hnm (v.)	to join (indicated as past tense)
hnp (v.)	to steal away
hnw (n.)	dwelling
hpr (n.)	being (as in Khepri)
hr (prep.)	on
Hrw (n.)	Horus
hs (n.)	a water charm
hsb (v.)	to calculate
ht (n.)	body
hti (v.)	graven
hw (n.)	utterance
hwa (n.)	rottenness
ib (n.)	heart
idbw (n.)	shore
imn (v.)	hidden
ini (v.)	to add
ir (n.)	a doer
iri (n.)	1.) hat; 2.) pilot
iri (v.)	to create (indicated as past tense)
isft (n.)	injustice or evil
iti (v.)	to subtract
iwty (adj.)	stupid; witless
ka (n.)	phenomenon
kai (adj.)	high/primeval mound

EGYPTIAN	TRANSLATION
kd (v.)	fashioned
kfa (n.)	a captive
kkw (n.)	darkness
kma (v.)	to create
Kmt (n.)	Egypt
kt (n.)	thing
m (indefinite article)	a
m (n.)	Shu
ma (adverbial phrase)	as at
maa (v.)	to see
mandt (n.)	the day-bark
mdt (n.)	word
mnfat (n.)	soldiers
mr (n.)	love
msa (n.)	masses (correlation)
msi (v.)	to be made or born
mwt (adj.)	mortem; of the dead
nb (n.)	possessor
nbi (v.)	to make (indicated as past tense)
nd (v.)	to protect
nfr (n.)	good
ngg (n.)	egg/stone (correlation)
nh (v.)	to escape
nhh (n.)	eternity
nhm (n.)	unconsciousness
niswt (n.)	politician
niwt (n.)	rock
nrt (adj.)	awful (title of Neith)
nsni.f (v.)	to rage (indicated as present tense)
ntr (n.)	god
ntri (v.)	to sanctify
nwn/nun (n.)	flood
nwt.j (n.)	town
pa dr (n.)	helper
pah (adj.)	rapacious

EGYPTIAN	TRANSLATION
pet (n.)	sky
phrt (n.)	refuge
pri (v.)	to emerge
pth (v.)	to sculpt (as in Ptah)
rdi (v.)	to have kept
rh (adj.)	knowing (sounds very similar to Ra/Re)
rmit (n.)	a tear
rmt (n.)	man
rnnt (n.)	upbringing
rs-wda (adj.)	healthy
sa (n.)	son
saa (v.)	to begin (indicated as past tense)
sah (v.)	1.) to be given; 2.) to step
sai (n.)	fate
sanh (v.)	to revive
sar (v.)	to ascend
sat (n.)	wall
sbayt (n.)	dharma; god's teaching
sdb (n.)	incrimination
shm (n.)	power
shwy (n.)	compendium
sia (n.)	perception (as in the goddess Sia)
smaw (adj.)	condensed
smd (adj.)	deep
smi (v.)	to find (indicated as past tense)
smn (adj.)	fixed
smr (v.)	cry or endure pain
snmh (n.)	prayer
snsn (v.)	to join
sprwt (n.)	petition
sr (n.)	prophet
ss (n.)	deed
ssm (v.)	to direct stars
sta (n.)	secret
stni (adj.)	different

EGYPTIAN	TRANSLATION
sw (n.)	sun
swn (v.)	to foresee (indicated as past tense)
ta (n.)	earth
thi (v.)	to sin (indicated as past tense)
tr (n.)	time
twa (adj.)	poor
ty lg (v.)	to expel (indicated as present tense)
wah (v.)	to endure
wawa (n.)	scheme
wbn (v.)	to rise
wd (n.)	commandment, as on stele
wdn (n.)	offerings
whm (n.)	messenger
wn (v.)	to be
wpt (n.)	separation
wpw (adj. phrase)	only that
wr (n.)	great
wsht (n.)	chamber
ym (n.)	the sea personified

PERSONIFICATION

In the Dead Sea Scrolls' Rule of Blessings, written circa 1000 B.C.E., the "Prince of the Congregation is praised, 'May you slay the wicked.... May God make your horns of iron and your hooves of bronze; may you gore like a bull and trample the Gentiles like mud in the streets."[v] The Apis, Mnevis and Buchis bulls of pharonic tradition and celestial cows like Baty, Ihet, Sekhat-Hor, and Hathor existed long in Egypt before this verse was written. Again, it is estimated that the incantations from *The Book of the Dead* began circa 3000 or 4000 B.C.E.[vi] Biblical writers adopted the same metaphors with all sorts of creatures.

The Egyptians had already founded the "significant theological concept... [that they had] accepted man yet did not reject the animal kingdom."[vii] In the Egyptian Ptolemaic Stela it is written that "a priest should mention his services in looking after and embalming sacred animals, in the same breath with his good moral conduct, as deserving divine reward."[viii] It is clear that Biblical authors drew parallels from related topics. Demonstrated here are parallels with Egyptian lion-gods and -goddesses such as Sekhmet, Pakhet, Shesmetet, and Tefnut, who became, as was traditional using their Egyptian definitions, associated with the wrath of the Israelite god.

> The lion killed enough for his cubs, and strangled the prey for his mate.... The Angry Lion who smites by his great ones and the men of his party, [filling with his kill, ladens] his lairs and his dens with prey, ...acts of revenge against the "seekers of smoothness", who hangs up men alive... in Israel.... For concerning one hanged alive on a tree, it says, "Behold, I am against you."[ix]

Many such comparisons may be made, such as the Hymn to Aten with Psalm 140 and the Maxims of Ptah-hotep with the Ten Commandments.[x] On the following pages are a few more examples, but it is certain that an exhaustive study of ancient Egyptian literature as compared with Biblical works would prove to be a rewarding and much-needed enterprise.

(Reference to *The Book of the Dead* is used here as a generality representing the broad-spectrum of both that work and traditional associated stories. Specific references may be found at the end of this book.)

MOTIFS

The Book of the Dead	The Bible
Put not thy trust in length of years; [the judges of the dead] regard a lifetime as an hour. A man remaineth over after death and his deeds are placed beside him in heaps.[xi]	Lay not up for yourselves treasures upon earth, where moth and rust doth corrupt, ...but lay up for yourselves treasures in heaven, where neither moth nor rust do corrupt.... For by grace are we saved, through faith, not of works, lest any man should boast.[xii]
Hail to you, King of Kings, Lord of Lords, Ruler of Rulers, who took possession of the Two Lands even in the womb of Nut; he rules the plains of the Silent Land, even he the gold body, blue of head, on whose arms is turquoise.[xiii]	He carried me away in the spirit to a great and high mountain, and showed me that great city, ...having the glory of God: and her light was like unto a stone most precious, even like a jasper stone...and the city was pure gold,... and the foundations... were garnished with all manner of precious stones.... And he that talked with me had a golden reed.[xiv]

Very rapture-like verbiage:
"You have not departed dead,
you have departed alive."[xv]

The Book of the Dead	**The Bible**

O you waxen one who take by robbery and who live on the inert ones, I will not be inert for you, I will not be weak for you, your poison shall not enter into my members, for my members are the members of Atum. If I am not weak for you, suffering from you shall not enter into these members of mine.[xvii]

And if thy right eye offend thee, pluck it out and cast it from thee: for it is profitable that one of thy members should perish, not that the whole body should be cast into hell.[xvi]

Your serpent-foe has been given over to the fire and the rebel serpent is fallen, his arms are bound, Re has taken away his movements.[xviii]

The serpent was more subtil than any beast of the field which the Lord God had made.... The Lord God said unto the serpent, Because thou hast done this, thou art cursed above... every beast of the field; upon thy belly shalt thou go, and... the great dragon was cast out, that old Serpent, called the Devil, and Satan, which deceiveth the whole world.[xix]

The Book of the Dead	The Bible
The hero... looks into the realm of the dead... [and] learns how, in accordance with a divine judgement, the pompous furnishings of a rich but unjust man's tomb are assigned to the poor but just man, who is buried in just fashion; the latter achieves happiness next to Osiris, while the rich man suffers the torments of hell.[xxi]	It is easier for a camel to go through the eye of a needle, than for a rich man to enter into the kingdom of God.[xx]
He says: O all you gods of the Soul-mansion who judge sky and earth in the balance... give praise to Re, Lord of the Sky, the sovereign who made the gods.... May a place be made for me in the solar bark on the day when the god ferries across, and may I be received into the presence of Osiris in the Land of Vindication.[xxiii]	Let not your heart be troubled: ye believe in God, believe also in me. In my Father's house are many mansions: if it were not so I would not have told you. I go to prepare a place for you.[xxii]

The Book of the Dead	The Bible
Worship of Osiris Wennefer, the Great God who [is]... King of Eternity, Lord of Everlasting... whose White Crown is tall, Sovereign of gods and men. He has taken the crook and the flail and the office of his forefathers.[xxiv]	The Lord is my shepherd; I shall not want.... Yea, though I walk through the valley of the shadow of death, I will fear no evil: for thou art with me; thy rod and thy staff they comfort me.[xxv]
O Pillar of Myriads, broad of breast, ... he the golden body... kindly of countenance, who is in the Sacred Land: May you... who took possession of the Two Lands... grant power in the sky, might on earth, and vindication in the realm of the dead....[xxvi]	For, behold, I have made this day a defended city, and an iron pillar, and brasen walls against the whole land, against the kings of Judah.... And they shall fight against thee; but they shall not prevail against thee; for I am with thee, saith the Lord, to deliver thee.[xxvii]

Specific classical themes recur. In Genesis 1: 15-21, Sarah and Abraham's desire to bring forth a son in spite of apparent barenness could well have been based on the story of Taimhotep and her husband. In both stories, God directs that sacrifices be made, after which time the couple shall receive their blessing.[xxviii]

In the Biblical version of this story, the son, Isaac, begets Jacob. Jacob and his family see visions in dreams, e.g., the famous "Jacob's ladder" motif. The Egyptian faithful also received such messages in dreams. Literary instances include notations in the Famine Stele where in order to cease death Khnum-Re Ptah appeared to Pharoah Zoser and offered him knowledge of the time of solace.[xxix]

As proselytes of any religion require instruction, institutions are significant. Literary and artistic merits, in addition to the benefits of long-lasting tradition, can only be maintained by a highly-organized and rigorously-knowledgable faculty. Egyptian lodges organized for this purpose became known to foreign visitors as the infamous "Egyptian Mystery System," and they were to become roughly equivalent to our universities.

III DISSEMINATION

40

THE EGYPTIAN MYSTERY SYSTEM

Since organized theological institutes may have originated in Egypt, it must be determined how knowledge was dispersed from one continent to another. As early as 650 B.C.E. Egypt was trading with Greece, as the Egyptians attempted to extend their sphere of influence as far and wide as possible. To the northeast, the Hittites and their allies, profoundly affected by Egypt, began to quickly imitate their hieroglyphs and sphynxes.[xxx] To the south, the citizens of cities such as Meroe, lost nome of ancient Sudan and Ethiopia, went so far as to build pyramids and make Egyptian their native language.

Senusret (1965-1920 BCE) extended Egypt's range to include India and the territory east to the Pacific Ocean. This explains not only India but also China's Egyptian influence indicated as from renderings of political mediation.[xxxi] George M. James suggests that the "ancient Grand Lodge of Luxor... built by Pharoah Amen[hotep] III... had branches or minor lodges throughout the ancient world" extending as far as Australia.[xxxii]

Yosef Ben Jochannen claims that Abraham was born in Ur in Chaldea circa 1675 B.C.E. "Before 1000 B.C.E., there was not any European writing — the first writing was Homer, and he said that Zeus and Apollo came from Ethiopia." These theories support that of George M. James in that university students went to Egyptian schools and then traveled elsewhere with missionary zeal. Their reputation became widely-known and "impressed Herotodus when he visited Egypt in about 450

B.C.[E.].... Homer in the Odyssey speaks of the Egyptians as 'sons of Paean all,' Paean being the physician of the Olympian gods.... The prophet Jeremiah also spoke of the country as 'the land of many medicines....'" Their practices were thus "carried out by the priesthood and were described by Heron, a Greek mathemetician of the second century B.C.[E.]"[xxxiii]

Graduates apparently had "doctorates" in the priesthood, which included healing both mental and physical illnesses. "Egypt abounded with sorcerers and magicians.... The Egyptian doctor was expected not only to cure his clients but to prevent snakes from entering their houses and to drive all vermin away."[xxxiv]

Johannen also finds that Imhotep practiced medicine in 2870 B.C.E., 2400 years before Hippocrates was credited with doing so. His thesis is that the Greeks and Europeans are credited with more than that which they actually have accomplished, which is probable.
Certainly, Egyptian texts support Johannen's facts.

Such educational institutions were established throughout Egypt's territorial extensions. Rumored is that famous spokesmen and prophets (Moses among them) attended such schools. The only "mystery" of Egyptian lodges is why they were labeled as such, for the teachings appear to have been clear, but only provided that the student was familiar with basic tenets.

Proper instruction would have included the hermeneutics of sacred texts, with phrasing such as, "as for Min, he is Horus who protected his father."[xxxv] Explanation: Osiris battled Seth, was injured, died and resurrected. Min, the god of mummies, or of "the living dead," preserved Osiris as did Horus, trying to protect his father. Like the language of *The Book of the Dead*, the explanation is the technical formula for speaking the "arithmetic" of that which could possibly be construed as an exemplary ancient Egyptian Mystery. The here chosen verbiage may be celebrated as preserving a well-thought-out sacred order which enlivens raw literary description by way of colorful storyline and background. In other words, the goal must have been memory-aid, where a suggested verbal idea conjures a mental picture.

In order to say that Min is Horus, who protected his father, one must know the stories of all three. It is like saying "Jesus, Mary, and Joseph" and automatically Roman Catholics visualize a manger in a stable full of hay and cattle. This requires not only extremely detailed knowledge on the part of anyone hearing such ceremonial words, but also invokes the idea that, while Egyptian visual art and writing are considered flat and static by today's standards, creative memorization had to have been facilitated in a way that can best be compared today only with "campfire stories" and oral tradition. This requires a great deal of influence and is thought-provoking in and of itself.

Aesthetics must have been supplemented by philosophy. It is well-known that not only was the pantheon detailed, but it linked complex concepts and god-names one to another. Akhenaten's sole god, Aten, was actually Re-Harakte, the falcon of Horus at his conception, and later became the sun disk.[xxxvi] Aten was thus the culmination of the scores of gods which had come before him and had been contrived as the ultimate deification of a substance or thought, also a characteristic of the Egyptian pantheon.

Deification as hermeneutics may have begun with the philosophically complex association of an untouchable divine ideal with things best recognized in daily life. Greek philosophers attempted to modify what was actually an Egyptian theological abstraction, as is evidenced in Plato's "World of Forms." A chart has been provided on the following pages in order to demonstrate the correlation between such ideals and some of their deified names.

Abstraction	Egyptian Nomen	Judaeo-Christian Nomen	Latin/Greek Nomen[xxx]
Abundance	Bahet		
Angel of the Night	Heqet	Lailah	Hecate
Baptism	Kebechet		
Being	Khepri		
Coma Bernices	Berenic		
Confusion	Rait	Babel	
Contention		Esek	
Coral		Ramoth	
Cow	Hathor		Io
Darkness	Kekt		
Desert	Seth		
Destruction/Sin	Ammit	Hormah	
Division		Peleg	
Dust		Adamah	
Earth	Geb	Bohu/Heled	
Education	Seshat		
Face of the Sun	Re	Peniel	Helios/Apollo
Falcon	Horus		Harpocrates
Fertility	Bast		
Fire		Esh	Prometheus
Fortune	Renenti		Fortuna
Heavens		Tohu	
Infinity	Hauhet		
Intelligence	Sia		
Isolation	Aasith		
Joy	Autyeb		
Judgment	Maat	Dinah	
Life	Ankh	Chavah	
Light	Khut		
Lion		Ariel	
Love	Ken		Eros
Magic	Heka		Khoemnis
Mercury	Sebeg		
Moon			Diana
Morality	Anubis		
Motherhood	Bat	Eve	
Mummification	Min		
Orion	Sakhmet	Cesil	
Pleiades		Cimah	
Politics	Onuris		
Pride		Rahab	
Primordial Orb		Adoil	

Abstraction	Egyptian Nomen	Judaeo-Christian Nomen	Latin/Greek Nomen[xxxvii]
Protection	Sekhet		
Seasons	Ahket		
Seed	Muyt		
Sirius	Sepedet/Isis		
Smoke		Chidon	
Spring Equinox		Nisan	
Strength		Boaz	
Sun's Path	Abetneterus		
Sunrise	Aasheft	Zarah	
Sunset Flame	Ahabit/Akusaa		
Sunshine	Ahat/Net		
Time	Atem		
Ursa Major	Kepha		
Vengefulness	Sekhmet	Sitnah	
War	Mafdet		Ares
Weather	Nebt		
Youth	Kebehut		
Zodiac		Mazzaroth	

Great leaders had to have not only religious knowledge as above, but also comprehensive scientific and botanical knowledge. The Ebers translation of the Kahun Papyrus, circa 2000 B.C.E., "contains seven hundred prescriptions.... The mineral remedies included a solution of ammonium hydroxide with the sulphates, carbonates, and oxides of several metals. Salts of copper may have been prescribed for ophthalmia which was always prevalent in their hot and sandy country. Sodium chloride, iron sulphate, and the oxides and carbonates of lead are all mentioned.... The vegetable remedies include onion, cara-way, mint, aloes, myrrh, colchicum, saffron, and cedar,... the pea and bean family, ...acacias, mimosas, and cassias...."[xxxviii] The Egyptians also used gum arabic, fig, flax and linseed oil.

"The blood of the ibis was frequently given, and we are told a great deal about the therapeutic value of precious stones."[xxxix] In this vein it is also probable to note that the Ben Ben Stone, an altar meant to catch the blood of the sacrificed, may have been used for such purposes. Since Benu was the name for god as a bird, it is not difficult to imagine that the Stone was used for this purpose. The ben, a spirit of the sun contained within the human body and related to the ba, could be released to heaven by means of submission on a Ben Stone. "The Ben Stone... was a short, thick obelisk which stood upon a base in the form of a truncated pyramid. On the east side of this sacred 'standing stone' was an altar on which victims were sacrificed, and on the north side were channels by which the blood was conducted into alabaster bowls placed in position to receive it."[xl] If Dr. Budge's statements are true, it is thus probable that the schools required knowledge of the justice system as well.

I have recently found it interesting to read of the relatively new findings regarding the construction of the pyramids. These are pertinent because of the intricate detail and exact positioning of burial places which would ensure resurrection in the next life. In fact, in order to mathematically prove the results to be mentioned below, the Egyptians would have to have done the following: compute the date when the right ascension of the two stars differed by exactly 180 degrees... [and] compute the minimum angular distance between the north celestial pole and the great circle passing through the pair of stars at 25-year intervals around these dates."[xli] For the Egyptians, precision meant the difference between life and death. If George M. James' theories are true, it is no wonder as to why Pythagoras studied here.

    New findings suggest that, in the second year of a pharoah's reign, he or she had an induction ceremony, the purpose of which was to design a burial place based on the positioning of the stars. "There was an elaborate 'fixing the north' ceremony... rather than a systematic sequence... over months or years...."[xlii] The movements of the stars and burial plot assignments were determined at the time of the rite. "Researchers proposing stellar methods agree that the Egyptians used northern or circumpolar stars for orientation, which suggests that the alignment ceremony was carried out for either the east or west side of the pyramid.... [Studies] suggest that only one side was accurately aligned and that it was the west side of the structure."[xliii] The side facing the realm of the dead, that pertaining to the afterlife, was the most accurate.

    "Can Egyptologists find references to such a ceremony in the ancient texts?... There is a text about two sharp claws chasing each other around the pole. Could this be an echo of Kochab and Mizar making their alignment rounds?"[xliv] The Big and Little Dippers do, coincidentally, form "hooks" around the pole between Kochab and Mizar.

    The two stars in particular that were used for the alignment were from the constellation which includes our Big Dipper, which is ancient Egypt's Adze. Encompassing the

Adze and the Little Dipper are the stars Kochab and Mizar. "Of the eight pyramids dating from 2600-2400 B.C.[E.,] six lie approximately in a straight line. The other two, the pyramids of Khafre and Sahure, lie close to this group."[xlv]

It becomes apparent that studies in the ancient Egyptian Mystery System consisted of the following: morality in sacred practice regarding both priestly conduct and interactions with the common people; oraculaar training (the ability to cause "mysteries," to interpret dreams, and to give counsel); an understanding of science, medicine, basic geology, methods of bodily preservation; and other allied arts and sciences, such as mathematics, astronomy, and philosophy. Certainly complex religious institutions would have been necessary in order to implement such training.

MAAT

Not only did the Egyptians share our national colors but they also shared another American symbol, The Statue of Liberty, in the sense that it personifies the Lady of Truth (weighing the scales) judging the moral affairs of the nation in an Anubis-like manner. Her guiding force of consciousness is Maat. (Goodness is female.)

The Ennead judged in heaven by means of Maat. The panel consisted of nine elders who had become gods, and were in fact similar to the Ogdoad, an original god-group of eight. A similar construction to the Ennead is given in The Book of Jubilees where "the righteous live a mythical existence and enjoy a prediluvian longevity of a thousand years or more. Their souls will enjoy immortality."[xlvi] (Similar are the Biblical four and twenty elders of Revelation.[xlvii] Longevity, in both modern Christian and ancient Egyptian cultures, appears to be written of as the benefit of a good relationship with God.)

Maat was the goddess of truth and right conduct; but what is particularly notable is that she is also known as consciousness. Therefore your every thought should be the wonderfully infectious goddess Maat.

Maat was represented by a feather, as was Thoth's wisdom. This probably has something to do with writing tools and education as well as avian freedom; "the freedom to go in and out," that is to traverse divine worlds, as in *The Book of the Dead*.

It is the attributes of people and gods which are god

names, but the ultimate NTR, or God, is the primary self produced producer and is also a quality which the gods possessed which was greater than the gods themselves. Using a definition of pure consciousness or essential energy such as the above, verses such as those in *The Book of the Dead* evoke a more Eastern feel like that of the Bhagavadgita or other Buddhist texts. These passages from *The Book of the Dead* are quoted by Budge:

1. Boy netri, heir or eternity, begetting and giving birth to himself.
2. I am devoted in my heart without feigning, O thou [of] netri more than the gods [the gods being referred to as neteru].
3. Shall be said this chapter over a crown of netrat.
4. I have become neter.
5. I have risen up in the form of a hawk['s] netri.
6. I have become pure, I have become neter, I have become a spirit, I have become strong, I have become a soul (ba).
7. His being neter with the gods in the [realm of] Neter-khertet.
8. He shall [make] netra his body all.
9. They make neter thy soul in the house of Sebut.
10. He makes neter thy soul like the gods.
11. God netri, self-produced, primeval matter.

In Verse 4 NTR appears to refer to the essential energy of enlightenment, that meditative "golden silence" esteemed by all cultures, particularly Zen Buddhism.[xlviii]

Philosophically speaking, one does not have to be identical to the god or strictly godly or godlike. One does not have to be metaphorically "created in God's image," as it were. If the concept of neter is beyond god, or that ultimate essential energy that is pure, like a hawk flying to the Osirian sky, then each individual part of the puzzle is essential. Each person should "make netra his body all," and it is this that "makes neter thy soul like the gods." Living rightly means that one is "devoted in [his/her] heart without feigning,... [to] netri" and in so doing can achieve "more than the gods."

IV REDEMPTION

THE JESUS/OSIRIS CONNECTION

The nexus of communion is personal fulfillment through renewal, most clearly expressed through a sacred prophet's resurrection. As Christians celebrate Jesus, Egyptians celebrated Osiris. Both unjustly-persecuted patriarchs, braving death for the glory of resurrection, attracted worshippers reenacting, or "going through the motions" of, their martyrdom. Known as experiencing "mysteries" (The Stations of the Cross are libations of this type), such involvement promotes both patronage and drama by reinforcing a Freudian system of punishment and reward.

Between the two evangelists there are vivid similarities. The divine son comes down from heaven. God came down to earth to guide the world: "I am Thoth, the eldest son of Re, whom Atum has fashioned... I descended to earth with the secrets of 'what belongs to the horizon'."[xlix] The aspects of his godliness are, in some way deified, a Christian example being *The Bible*'s Sofia, or Wisdom, and an Egyptian example being Thoth — female and male aspects of the same principle: "wisdom crieth without; she uttereth her voice in the streets."[l]

The Son of God appears on earth borne of woman through union of the human species and the divine. Osiris' and Jesus' were paracletic virgin births, and while "the immaculate conception" has been deemed to be a Medieval idea, the premise is actually an ancient one; "In Queen Hatshepsut's mortuary temple at Deir el-Bahari, and in one of the halls built by Amen[hotep] III in the temple of Luxor, ...God, in the guise of the pharoah, is shown approaching the woman thus blessed."[li] Y.B. Jochannen asserts that the Immaculate Conception is also shown 4000 years before Roman history in the Temple of Seti I at Abydos. The divine son appeared borne of human parents, forming a trinity: Isis, Osiris and Horus, and Mary, Joseph, and Jesus.

Jesus and Osiris, though just men, were betrayed by dinner-guests (Jesus by Judas, and Osiris by Typhon) at their own privately-held banquets. Osiris was 28; Jesus was 23. Wooden trunks became their instruments of death as well as their memorials. Upon death, their bodies were wrapped by Isis and Mary in linens, anointed with oil, and entombed. The deaths of the Sons of Man were reverberated on earth in the manifestation of strange natural phenomena.

Osiris and Jesus were shortly resurrected. Reassuming earthly form, they demonstratively reaffirmed right conduct and its other-worldly rewards, after which time they returned to heaven, both having "saved the world."

Regarding assumptions and ascensions, it is interesting to note that the uniquely Egyptian transcendent idea is not alien to Chinese literature. In Chinese myth Jingwei was the soul-bird, an example of the ba concept in ancient Egypt, which rose from danger (in this case, during the Great Flood) and flew to heaven.[lii] This uniquely Egyptian transcendent idea is not alien to Chinese literature. Modern Christianity retains a similar belief in the form of assumptions and ascensions since the soul is transferred to a supernatural body which then rises up to heaven.

THE MARY/ISIS CONNECTION

Y.B. Jochannen suggests that Jesus was born in a cave in Ethiopia. The Coptics, however, under the Emperor Constantine, changed the story and created the idea of a manger in Bethlehem. He also alleges that the Black Madonna, still an essential symbol in Roman Catholicism, moved to Greece as the Herculean worship of Isis.

It is interesting to note here that there is some evidence to support the theory that both Mary and Jesus were Egyptian in origin. I would like to stress that this is not about skin color; my college professor, Ira Spar, said that Egyptians painted all men as red and all women as yellow. They were not concerned with skin color, and therefore, why should we be? I have seen photographs of Egyptian royal mummies with red hair, of European origin, as well as much evidence which points to a purely dark African origin. Surely, all colors existed in that environment at some point, and it was the citizenry of Egypt that was important.

In any event, other findings support the herein facts, but are of later date. The Christian Roman Catholic Biblical and Apocryphal book Bel and the Dragon, for example, written in the second century B.C.E., seems to have certainly been used as reference material for today's common Bible, particularly the Book of Revelation in the New Testament, which was written circa C.E. 95. The ancient origins of Bel and the Dragon as part of the Christian Apocrypha are historically acknowledged; "the author was ridiculing, in typical early Jewish literary fashion, the two main characters of the Babylonian creation myth, the *Enuma Elish,* Bel or Marduk, and Tiamat, a sea serpent or monster whom Marduk slew as the major act of creation."[liii] There is a tradition of verses such as these.

Now in that place there was a great dragon, which the Babylonians revered, [and] the king said to Daniel,"...I give you permission... to kill the dragon without sword or club...." He fed... the dragon, [who] ate them, and burst open.[liv]

I purpose to describe her divine semblance.... Her vestment was of finest linen yielding diverse colours, somewhere white and shining, somewhere yellow like the crocus flower, somewhere rosy red, somewhere flaming.... Round about the whole length of the border of that goodly robe was a crown.... An asp lifted up his head with a wide-swelling throat. "I am she that is the natural mother of all things, mistress and governess of all the elements, the initial progeny of worlds, chief of the powers Divine, queen of all,... the Mother of the Gods.... Do call me by my true name, Queen Isis."[lv]

And there appeared a great wonder in heaven: a woman clothed with the sun, and the moon under her feet, and upon her head a crown of twelve stars: And she being with child cried, travailing in birth, and pained to be delivered. And there appeared another wonder in heaven: and behold a great red dragon.... And there was war in heaven:... and the great dragon was cast out, that old serpent.[lvi]

An unlikely virgin becomes associated with motherhood and the dragons of glory, as her son goes on to become God. (Coincidentally, there is a more minute theme of Isis finding Osiris in the water under a tamarisk tree, which reminds me — and Y.B. Jochannen — of the story of baby Moses floating down the river.) It is easy to see that Mary and Isis play identical roles in the modern Christian and ancient Egyptian schemes.

V THE IMPORTANCE OF THE EIGHTEENTH DYNASTY

AKHENATEN

Although we hear it frequently rumored that Pharoah Akhenaten should be credited with the introduction of monotheism to Egypt, the inherent concepts were already present in the culture. Akhenaten's revolution, not unlike the Reformation, began with the stress on the personal aspect of god's relationship. God was Time, Life and Death, and He/She would save souls through grace as is Biblical and the belief of Born-Again Christiandom and Protestantism.

Predestination establishes another link with Protestantism. "The Instruction for Merikare states that God created for [hu]man[ity] 'rulers from the womb.'"[lvii] (There are, of course, many other examples, but I cite one simply as proof of the statement.)

The Pharoah Akhenaten brought the Personal Jesus aspect of Protestantism to the forefront. By latest estimates, Akhenaten was a small and slender man of between 35 and 40, and his portrayals have given rise to the theory that he may have endured Marfan's syndrome, but he certainly possessed a rare appearance.[lviii]

Brier, in his analysis of Akhenaten, explained that he revised his "view of Akhenaten: he wasn't a freak. You can look different without looking freakish."[lix]

If Akhenaten was affected with a genetic condition that altered his appearance and made him look unusual (Marfan's Syndrome is just one of many suggested afflictions,) why would "he permit court sculptors to show his physical characteristics?"

> For more than a thousand years pharoahs had been portrayed as young, well-muscled, and perfect, no matter what they looked like. Akhenaten could have stayed with the traditional art style and been portrayed slim and well-muscled like his ancestors before him. He chose not to and the entire royal family followed suit. Why? I think the answer is a psychological one.[lx]

Brier indicates that Akhenaten may have been trying to make a case for people with Marfan's syndrome, a.k.a., indicating that its victims were "as good as anyone else". This, while possible, does not explain why pharoahs with other conditions — even as familiar as obesity— did not in any other epoch find it necessary or acceptable to portray themselves as such to as great a degree; and certainly this would have been more readily accepted. It stands to reason that if Akhenaten *was* making a psychological statement, then the statement would have to be greater than his family's physical appearance if he would have wanted it universally expressed.

Previously considered relevant only in terms of the artistic workmanship during his reign, it may also be that Akhenaten was interested in bringing Horus-Isis language into the forefront of his doctrine, where male gods could be referred to in the context of goddess worship.

This may be the true reason for the unique art of his reign, where Re was no longer the static, circular ball of the sun that he had previously been. Re as Aten was shown with his arms and hands reaching out to people and giving them ankhs and lotus flowers.

Akhenaten, divine god-man of slender build, perhaps not well-muscled but attractive nontheless, is everywhere portrayed as a man with attractive feminine characteristics. In fact, when his body was discovered, it was believed to be that of his mother, Queen Tiye, for many years. If this is involved in any religious aspects of the Eighteenth Dynasty, there should be archeological evidence to indicate that the writings of the period took on a more singularly procreative quality.

Such evidence does exist. Since the gods and goddesses in the pantheon were often interchangeable as far as sex was concerned — "Horus the son of Isis. He has become ruler over Egypt, the gods work for him, he has nurtured myriads and has brought up myriads by means of the Sole Eye, the Mistress of the Enneads, the Lady of All."[lxi] — it then becomes evident that there is a stress on the sexually-unified Universal One, especially during the reign of Akhenaten. Biblical texts such as The Odes of Solomon also include this tendency; "the Holy Ghost opened the Father's raiment and mingled the milk from the Father's two breasts."[lxii]

It is believed that Akhenaten began his reign with a co regent, his predecessor Amenhotep III. Before Akhenaten's mummy was correctly dated, the reason for co-regency was believed to be Akhenaten's youth, indicating that he would have died by the time he had reached 25 or 30.

However, with Akhenaten's age at death now known as between 35 and 40, Amenhotep III's co-regency for the first twelve years of Akhenaten's reign served no purpose other than a "trinitarian" one, that a deity who is potentially unacceptable can be made acceptable through association with a tried and true absolute. There are also theories that Akhenaten's brother, Smenkhare, could have acted as co-regent for a few months of his reign.[lxiii] (There are other theories as well, which will be addressed later.)

Either Akhenaten was not ready accepted because of improper divine lineage (which is doubtful,) or, because of such substantial differences during the time of his reign, that his policies would not be accepted. Since Akhenaten was direct descendant of legitimate Queen Tiye the latter must be the case.

"In Akhenaten's new religion, ...only the king and his immediate family had direct access to the god. The ordinary man and woman could only worship through them."[lxiv] This sounds suspiciously like the Protestant and Biblical tenet that "there is only one mediator between god and man, [that is,] Jesus Christ."[lxv]

"Dramatic change in front of all Egyptians — a farmer in a village will say, 'this is crazy.' A priest will say, 'I will kill him.... The whole country was going against this man, but this man, Akhenaten, was supported by one powerful lady, Nefertiti."[lxvi] Substantial evidence of such change is indicated by study of his wife's portrayals and her *shabti* (the wooden statues which looked like you and were made to do any necessary work for you in the afterlife.)

Nefertiti's shabti have been mysterious because they portray her with the royal crook and flail — a king's right— but not in the dress of the king adopted by Hatshepsut during her pharoahship. Nefertiti has also been portrayed wearing the un-traditional ram's horns.[lxvii] Although theories as to her co-regency have sprung up from time to time it was established that Nefertiti could not have been co-regent because it was "inconceivable that an anointed and consecrated ruler with a distinctive prenomen and nomen, and a king's titles, would not have retained such honors after death and burial."[lxviii]

But why would a loyal wife and queen with king's titles, knowing that her "divine" husband had difficulties ascending the throne, usurp that which he had spent over twelve years trying to attain? If she had firmly believed in Akhenaten (she was at the very least "a great queen, loyal to his teachings") then a show of regnal dominance would have been an affirmation of his right to both theory and throne; one god, one leader, one uniform authority. She may well have ruled with Akhenaten as his aide, and not his competition.[lxix]

However, there is also the recently-developed idea that Nefertiti, like Hatshepsut, ruled independently. The above findings would seem to indicate this, however, publications such as National Geographic Magazine read as if she ruled only under the guise of the name Smenkhare. This means, then, that either there was no Smenkhare, or that he was a political puppet, and neither explanation appears plausible. If, on the other hand, with the support of Smenkhare, Akhenaten did allow his wife Nefertiti to rule either single-handedly or alongside him, no threats to the throne would exist.

NEFERTITI

The feminization of Akhenaten in artwork has been radically viewed, and whether or not Akhenaten had Marfan's Syndrome or other condition, he certainly sought to minimize the differences between himself and Nefertiti. Perhaps this was in order to glorify her and promote her to the level of pharoah. To compare himself visually, in a most important way, to the people on a level with Nefertiti, would have promoted her pharonic right.

This movement appears to have given rise to diminished patriarchy at this time (although not confined to the period), which may have affected the status of the gods. All of these changes were, unfortunately for Akhenaten, connected with his rise and fall. Upon his death, burial, and excavation out of the tomb, Akhenaten's body had been smashed with rocks, moved, its gold mask removed and used instead on his son, Tutunkhamen. His counterpart bust, as Nefertiti had possessed, had its face demolished, so that he could not breathe, eat, view, or in any way enjoy the blessings of the afterlife — an expression of absolute hatred.

Nefertiti's most famous counterpart bust, however, remains beautiful to this day, relatively untouched. Clearly the Egyptians did not mind having a female pharoah; what they did mind was the restructuring of the entire religious system, notably the striking-down of the old gods in favor of the One, Aten. Also objectionable was the idea that there was one pharonic mediator between god and man, and therefore the common people were not privy to communication with God.

Nefertiti was apparently a very clever and powerful woman. From the start of her independent reign she re implemented the old gods and gained the common people's favor.[lxx] This may be why her name may have changed to Smenkhare, a complete turnabout from the Neferneferaten that preceded Nefertiti. She appears to have played along with Akhenaten's ideas while ruling as queen, but when promoted to pharoah, reinstituted the old gods of her own choosing.

Since Akhenaten ruled with Nefertiti, there was a coincidental move to portray both man and woman with the same curves in the artwork and in the literature. The idea of national unification was all-encompassing with regard to the indivisibility of the Throne of Upper and Lower Egypt, and unity in all regards was of national concern.

Nefertiti held the common favor throughout her reign and beyond. "We see her wearing the kinds of headdresses that only pharoahs are shown with. We see her performing the kinds of actions that only pharoahs are shown doing.... I believe that she was... the most powerful lady in ancient Egypt because she took [up] one role that was only connected with kings, which is [to be] shown smiting an enemy."[lxxi] Even if she was not entirely autonomous, Nefertiti was certainly a highly-influential religious and political force in the ancient world.

VI CONSEQUENCES

ROLES OF WOMEN

Egyptian women held certainly greater power than in other cultures of the time. High positions were not easily granted but once attained were easily maintained, as exemplified to the greatest degree during this period of Egyptian history; i.e., Hatshepsut, Queen Tiye, Ankhsenamen, and Nefertiti.

Wives of all classes held the purse-strings; if a woman were disgraced by her husband he lost the share of the monetary assets with which she would come into the marriage house. A woman could, at least to some degree, select her husband.

This was exemplified by Nefertiti's attempt, after Akhenaten's death, to secure for herself a husband in Zennanza, son of the Hittite king Suppiluliumas. It has been suggested that this act was treasonous on Nefertiti's part, and the reason why Zennanza was assasinated on his way to Egypt for his bridal affair. Yet, the common people remained loyal to Nefertiti; it did not destroy her image, long after her death. It appears from this evidence that it was not the requisition of a husband that was disallowed, but possibly the fact that he was not a native Egyptian, and therefore he was killed before he had a chance to set foot on Egyptian soil.

Nefertiti may have been able to implement additional changes as well. Rank suddenly took matrilineal precedence in the Eighteenth Dynasty; "in the Eighteenth Dynasty the line of inheritance was by the eldest son of a king by a God's Wife, who was a descendant of Ahmose-Nefertari, the chief queen of Amosis, founder of the dynasty."[lxxii]

RELIGIOUS CENSORSHIP

Presented in the previous chapters is a more effective explanation as to why Akhenaten's beliefs were not universally accepted. Everything was in question; not only the gods, but also the religious, official, and traditional views of the people.

> The smaller, unofficial objects tell the true story at Amarna. For example, if we look at this [specimen in the Cairo museum of a] scarab of King Amenhotep III (which was found at Amarna,) we see that the name Amon has been excised in what I can only suppose is a fearful form of self-censorship. It was obviously not wise to be caught in possession of objects bearing the name of the hated god, Amon. This [excising] clearly wasn't done by Akhenaten's official agent because, although officially issued, this piece was ultimately privately owned. This shows us the true climate at Tel Amarna, and, for me, it was a climate of fear.[lxxiii]

Akhenaten must have had a powerful set of political enforcers in the priesthood who would, in an Inquisition-like manner, ensure worship of the true god. By the beginning of Tutunkhamum's succeeding reign, a new priesthood had to be appointed. Perhaps the coverts had not been sufficiently effective during Nefertiti's reign. In any event, the movement was strikingly threatening.

VII TALL TALES

GENESIS

 Aten created all by means of the sun and the sun's rays. He is the Old Testament's "Sun of Righteousness."[lxxiv] He "'came into being' before the creation," as is evident in Genesis, and "refers to his original state... [as] 'not yet,' which characterizes what is chaotic and shapeless all over the earth: 'Heaven had not yet come into being, the earth had not come into being, the creatures of the earth [and] the reptiles had not been made in that place.'"[lxxv]

 Creation accounts develop life from a chaotic physical object in its first form: a stone or an egg.[lxxvi] "The primordial egg is occasionally referred to as having been laid by a primeval bird: 'the egg of the great cackler....'"[lxxvii]

 This is comparable to the Big Bang evolutionary theory in that the cosmos arose from the explosive divison of an orbed mass. These developments took place during a lengthened creation time rather than in *The Bible*'s interpretable "days."

 If the egg is the primary material out of which life sprung, then the Egyptians' other theory may be considered a subset of it; life from a lotus. It seems to have arisen later in Egyptian history, but may have gained ground in China. The lotus sprung from Nun, the primeval ocean.[lxxviii] The egg, stone, and the lotus, which begins as a bud or a ball, are all the "primeval mounds" from which life arose.

 "The earth was without form and void; and darkness was upon the face of the deep[;]... the face of the waters."[lxxix] The concept of Nun existed in *The Bible* in the sense of its definition, a chaotic ocean to which the sun goes when it sets as Ahabit.

 "God said, Let there be light: and there was light. And

God saw the light... [and] divided the light from the darkness.... And the evening and the morning were the first day."[lxxx] Day and night settled into Nun in accordance with Egyptian rites.

Atum then created Shu and Tefnut, air and moisture. In both creation accounts, Nun is the root since it is out of Nun that the earth and sky are created, Geb and Nut.

On the second day, "God said, Let there be a firmament in the midst of the waters. And God made the firmament and divided the waters which were under the firmament from the waters which were above the firmament and it was so. And God called the firmament heaven."[lxxxi] Here the sky was separated from the rest of creation as Nut. Associated with rebirth and baptism, Akhet held humanity as Nut in the vault of heaven. (Heavenly spirits were reborn upon death and would become stars, or akhu.) The waters in heaven, the Field of Rushes, were separated from the waters on the earth in a division supported by pillars. The Biblical pillars were called in Egypt the Supports of Shu.

"God said, Let the waters under the heaven be gathered together unto one place, and let the dry land appear: and it was so."[lxxxii] This is Geb's first appearance. The sky and the dry land are separated.

> Now the land... presented a scene of prosperity. Spring, summer, autumn and winter came in turn. The whole universe was in perfect order.... There were no beasts, birds, insects or serpents but that concealed their claws and ceased to discharge their poisons. [There were no] vicious hearts to do harm to the human race. Food plants grew everywhere on the plains.... Free from care, people of the "central plains"... lived an easy, blissful life.[lxxxiii]

The concept of the Garden of Eden exists in these belief systems as a perfect, ideal world in which to place the new creation, humanity. In the Tale of Re and Sekhmet, Re created a parallel perfect world where flora and fauna flourished in peace.

> And the Lord God made to grow every tree that is pleasant to the sight and good for food, the tree of life also in the midst of the garden, and the tree of the knowledge of good and evil....[lxxxiv]

This tree is perhaps the most prominent feature in the Garden. "Immortality trees" are mentioned in *The Stories from Chinese Mythology (I)* and hold the clandestine prospect for either destroying the one who partakes of its fruit (Eve in *The Bible*, the Lady Changè in Chinese myth) or for making the individual "ascend to heaven and become a god."[lxxxv]

Once land and sustenance were created, humanity was born. God took a stroll in the world which he had created and ascertained what was missing.

> One day, Nu Wa was strolling on the vast plains.... [and] a sense of loneliness overcame her. She felt that something needed to be added to the universe to make it thrive and prosper.... [Nu Wa] dug a handful of clay from the brink of the pond and mixed it with water. She rolled the clay into a ball in her hand and moulded the first ball into a little thing like a baby.... No sooner [had it] touched the ground than it came to life and shouted: "Mama!"[lxxxvi]

Egyptian creation by the hands of Khnum-Ptah was almost as tender as the Chinese parable. Man was lovingly formed by hand on God's potter's wheel, made of clay and straw. *The Bible* was matter-of-fact regarding such things — "Male and female he created them..." When the incident is echoed in Jeremiah 18: 3-6; "I went down to the potter's house, and behold, he wrought a work on the wheels. And the vessel that he made of clay was marred in the hand of the potter: so he made it again another vessel, as seemed good to the potter to make it. Then the word of the Lord came to me, saying, O house of Israel, cannot I do with you as this potter? saith the Lord. Behold, as the clay is in the potter's hand, so are ye in mine hand, O house of Israel."[lxxxvii]

Creation occurred in the Biblical and Egyptian gardens through the act of naming. The responsibility was given by God to the caretaker of the Garden. "God formed every beast of the field, and every fowl of the air; and brought them unto Adam to see what he would call them: and whatsoever Adam called every living creature, that was the name thereof."[lxxxviii] Surely this designation by name could not be deemed wrong since it is a prerequisite for existence. Egyptians, if guilty of anything, are only at fault for following this verse to a tee.

> And the Lord God commanded the man, saying,
> You may freely eat of every tree of the garden;
> but of the tree of the knowledge of good and evil
> you shall not eat, for in the day that you eat of it
> you shall die.[lxxxix]

The Biblical and Egyptian chronicles recount the beginning of mortality. "The man and his wife heard the sound of Yahweh God walking in the garden in the cool of the day, and they hid from Yahweh God among the trees of the garden."[xc]

While humanity was not made ashamed and embarrassed of awareness in the Tale of Re and Sekhmet, the couple did commit the sin of hubris, arrogance and forgetfulness of god. Re determined that they should be forever reminded so that humanity would no longer disrespect him or the environment which he had created. In an almost Sodom and Gomorrah-like expression of anger, Re sent the goddess Sekhmet to set them straight.[xci]

THE GREAT FLOOD

The Book of the Dead, Pyramid Texts, Mesopotamian *Gilgamesh Epic, The Bible*, and other Oriental creation accounts include tales of a Great Flood, where spiritual birds return live branches as proof that the flood has subsided. Birds represented the freedom to go in and out, that is to traverse the other world and yet return safely from divinity or danger.

Thus evil beasts could be conquered by such a flight to heaven. Re as the sun-disk could take the shape of a benu-bird if he so chose, and the transfer of spirit in the flight of the bird was associated with his ascendance to the next life. Re's human souls could rise as bas and fly to the Field of Rushes.

While the Egyptian language united the religious with the avian (as with the ba, the heron as benu bird, and hawks, kites, eagles and vultures as symbols of the Heavenly Sun,) the Old Testament noted but reversed the idea in canonical lists of Leviticus and Deuteronomy, whereby birds that may have been worshipped were designated as unclean and/or not to be eaten; "The lapwing is there mentioned as an unclean, that is to say tabooed, bird in the distinguished company of the eagle, the griffon-vulture, the ibis, the cuckoo, the swan, the kite, the raven, owl and little owl, the solan-[or]... barnacle goose, the stork, the heron and the pious pelican.... Biblical scholars have been puzzled by the 'un cleanness' of the lapwing... and doubt whether the bird *is* a lapwing and not a hoopoe". Deuteronomy's list includes a bird called the glede. Also mentioned are the nighthawk and nightjar, the osprey, the hawk, the cormorant. It may be noted that the arbitrariness of these lists is augmented by the fact that they close with the words, "and the bat".[xcii]

XII GENERAL PRACTICES

THE SEVEN SACRAMENTS

Unction

The prefix heka- evolved into the Latin Magicus, the derivative of which the word magi was formed. Magi were Zoroastrian priests, and the story of the magi's arrival during the birth of Christ is somewhat of a Biblical acceptance of Zoroastrianism. Related is the philosophy whereby heka as a phenomenon made it possible from a religious standpoint to transfer energy from one person or thing to another by means of an object. This may even be indicated in the Biblical story through the presentation of the three
gifts of gold, frankincense and myrrh.

The tradition has survived throughout Judaeo-Christian times, and it finds expression today primarily in unction. For example, it is still acceptable for the dead to be buried with items of personal fondness; and during a funeral ceremony Hebrews cast soil on a casket as more than a reminder of "ashes to ashes, dust to dust" — there is an attempt to convey a last emotive energy with that soil.

The same heka is involved in memorializing a grave with flowers, where the presentation is a concrete wish for the body to remain spiritually preserved through a physical sign.

Such maintenance occurred then, as now, through visitation of the memorials.

Baptism

Heka can be imbued through a structure and it follows then that spiritual immersion with and in sacred material increases the propensity for divinity. This explanation accounts for mummification as well as baptism, that spiritual immersion with and in sacred material increases the propensity for divinity. This is an explanation for mummification as well as baptism.

Baptism in Egyptian times was a privilege deigned to be given only to royals. Blessed waters "poured from four gold vases" sanctified the pharoahs, priests and priestesses. [xciii]

Communion

As previously discussed, Biblical writers quickly learned that they could borrow Egyptian verbiage and maxims in order to describe and give a solid foundation to their "new" religion.[xciv]

> What, for the early Church Councils, seemed the most diabolical and unpardonable heresy of all was the identification of the Hercules-Dionysus-Mithras bull, whose living flesh the Orphic ascetics tore and ate in their initiation ceremony, with Jesus Christ whose living flesh was symbolically torn and eaten in the Holy Communion.... This heresy... was second-century Egyptian....[xcv]

The eucharist was neither a new idea nor was it novel to associate it with the god of the Israelites.

Confirmation

In one sense, confirmation may include any traditions which have the sole purpose of reinforcing beliefs in the current divinity's status on earth. The Sed Festival serves one such purpose in ancient Egypt. Once a year the king donned a white robe, jogged outside as a demonstration of his virility and potency in front of the people, and this was performed within the scope of a most honorable temple service which used an entire courtyard for the purpose. This would serve to renew individual interest in the reign from year to year and to motivate new followers.

Penance

The need for absolution and resolution was often practiced in the ancient world through conversation with a priest, as it is today. However, the forum was often of another nature. In the Grecian world, oracles were common. A citizen could go to the oracle and communicate with the god via the priest as mediator.

In Pharonic times, one could visit a priest or priestess outside near the temple, who would interpret one's dreams and/or resolve difficulties. In short, the functions in ancient societies were virtually identical to those in modern times.

Holy Orders

Characteristics of the Clergy and Parishoners

◊ Egyptian priests had podia for prepared speeches to be delivered in the temples and elsewhere.[xcvi]

◊ The Egyptians kept religious, aesthetic relics at home as well as in church. They even had fold-out tryptiches which celebrated miraculous deeds.

◊ Clergy have always been sure to make both their imagery and statuary realistic. The Egyptians painted both humans and animals as we do, inserted eyes and made the drama as true-to life as it is today.

◊ Statues were imbued with the spirit of the living god — not a wild idea or one beyond modern times. If one spends enough time at a Roman Catholic Church it is easy to see how many statues have their feet kissed by worshippers or have flowers placed upon them.

◊ "Egyptian sculpture, which served... religious needs... [was, by the New Kingdom,] elevated to an independent aesthetic plane: inscriptions by visitors praise the beauty of monuments in tourist fashion."[xcvii]

Priests are required to study and recall their canons and may use them to support the existence of miracles, most of which are fictitious. In the ancient world, shock value or the element of surprise was ofted credited with magic.

There is little oracular difference between the masculine bread and wine's transformation in monstrance and cup into the literal body and blood of Christ than there is in the following Egyptian rendering; an earthenware pitcher, molded with feminine features, was uniquely crafted so that the pitcher could be used in the normal manner unless needed for display. At that point, a mechanism could be pressed which would release the contents of the pitcher through the breasts of the goddess — one of many ready-made miracles.

THE LAYING ON OF HANDS

Holy Sanctified could, if blessed by Amen-Re, work wonders such as the restoration of health to mortally-ailing children. Such incidents, portrayed in memorial stelae from Thebes, remind one of Biblical verses such as Luke 7: 12-16 where Jesus performs similar acts; i.e., the "laying-on of hands" was not uncommon.[xcviii] "In the Genesis Apocrypon from the Dead Sea Scrolls, Abram heals the Pharaoh by laying hands on his head, thus proving that this New Testament 'innovation' existed earlier and was recorded in earlier scriptures."[xcix]

Marriage

This topic (discussed in the chapter on The Roles of Women) certainly verifies the existence of the sacrament and details its religious influence.

USE OF PALM BRANCHES

It was Egyptian tradition that the honorable be rewarded by their peers and kinsfolk by "the waving of palm fronds and olive branches".[c] This activity is Biblically documented in Mark 11: 6-10 and lasts until this day in Palm Sunday Catholic tradition.

ANGELS

The spirit of god, a female spirit known as the Hebrew Ruah and traditionally equated with breath and wind, created by "moving upon the waters." In the second century B.C.E.'s Jewish Book of Jubilees, spirits were created on the first day in a Druidic or Celtic manner. "On the first day he created the tall heavens and the earth and waters and all the spirits who served him: the angels of the presence, the angels of sanctification, the angels of the spirit of fire, the angels of the spirit of the winds, of the clouds, of darkness, of snow, hail, and hoarfrost, the angels of the voices of thunder and lightning, the angels of the spirits of cold and heat, of winter, spring, autumn, and summer, and of all spirits of his creatures in Heaven and on the earth."[ci] Indeed, spirits had to have been created first in order to create the breath of life and to "move the waters." [cii]

The seraphim and cherubim of which Roman Catholics sing in the hymn "Salve Regina" are based on Middle Eastern combatant omnipotent beings. It is this martial origin which is conveniently forgotten today, since it does not appear to fit with modern interpretations, e.g., warrior angels with swords who are associated with fire and the defense of the Gates of Heaven.

THE GATES OF SAINT PETER

The Egyptian soul is composed of the ba, ka and the akh at death when the soul becomes enlightened. The ka has been called one of the infinite mysteries of ancient Egypt. The ka is a facet of the soul which could be characterized as a double self; a living **conscience** within each person. The ka performs the same actions as the being because it *is* him or her, however, it may think differently and express a different opinion upon death.

If we were faced with the Gates of Hell, let's hope that our kas spoke up for us. The ka should say, "I know that N. is a good person because he/she has followed Maat (Righteousness)." The ka speaks for you in the next life but lives with you in this one. It knows all of your actions by the time you arrive in the next world. When you meet your Maker, there is one who intercedes on your behalf to the Panel at the Gate, if your moral behavior on earth was worthy.

The ka experiences your emotions and has your name. It cannot exist without you. One's ka can leave him or her if it finds that person repulsive because in texts such as Spell 110, it is a privilege to have a ka, and not an absolute right — "Hail to you, you owners of kas!" The ka may live forever in heaven, and the soul may traverse the worlds as a ba with the ka's permission. Thus permission must be granted to "go in and out," but it is achieved due to these two soul-aspects created by Re.

CONCLUSION

    It is impossible to speak of Plato, Aristotle, and the schools of thought associated with classical thinkers without also speaking of the ancient Egyptian school of thought as well. Egyptian disregard has resulted in gross theological misunderstanding. We have traced the routes of humankind's knowledge out of Africa and must also recognize the northern part of the continent as the seat from which religion sprang.

    It is disappointing that with one original way of life we have produced so many sects which are constantly at war with one another, be they evolutionary offshoots such as Islam and Judaism or sects within Christianity itself, such as Born-Again Christiandom, Protestantism, Roman Catholicism, Episcopalianism, Methodism, etc.

    To believe in your own system outweighing all others in terms of moral or hermeneutic value is unjust. *The Bible* states that "if any man among you seem to be religious, and bridleth not his tongue, but deceiveth in his own heart, this man's religion is vain. Pure religion and undefiled religion before God and the Father is this, To visit the fatherless and widows in their affliction, and to keep himself unspotted from the [uncleanliness in the] world."[ciii]. Remember that St. Paul said:

> I think myself happy... because I shall answer for myself.... My manner of life from my youth which was at first among mine own nation at Jerusalem, know all the Jews, which knew me from the beginning, if they would testify, that after the most straitest sect of our religion I lived a Pharisee. And now I stand and am judged for the hope of the promise of God made unto our fathers....[civ]

The message of the Bible is unification and not division. The true message of this book, in addition to its expansion of the Theological Canon, is an attempt to eleminate unneccessary derision and to bring "almost the whole city together to hear the word of God."[cv]

BIBLIOGRAPHY

Aldred, C. *Akhenaten: King of Egypt.* New York, NY: Thames and Hudson; 1988, 1991, 1994.

Barnstone, E., ed. *The Other Bible: Ancient Alternative Scriptures.* HarperSanFrancisco, a Division of Harper Collins Publishers of New York; 1984.

Brier, B. *The Murder of Tutankhamen: A True Story.* New York, NY: G.P. Putnam's Sons; 1998.

Budge, E. A. *The Gods of the Egyptians or Studies in Egyptian Mythology.* Volume I. First published London: Methuen & Co; 1904; Chicago, IL: The Open Court Publication Co; Toronto, Ontario: General Publication Co, Ltd; London; Constable and Co., Ltd; Mineola, NY: Dover Publications, Inc; 1969.

Cook, E.M. *Solving the Mysteries of the Dead Sea Scrolls: New Light on the Bible.* Grand Rapids, Michigan: Zondervan Publishing House, a Division of Harper Collins Publishers; 1994.

[Documentary]. The Learning Channel; Dec 6, 2000.

Faulkner, R.O., trans. *The Ancient Egyptian Book of the*

Dead. Andrews C, ed. First published New York, NY: The Limited Editions Club; 1972; Austin, TX: University of Texas Press in cooperation with British Museum Press; revised 1985, 1993.

Graves, R. *The White Goddess,* amended and enlarged edition. New York, NY: first published by International Authors N.V., reprinted by The Noonday Press, a Division of Farrar, Straus and Giroux; 1948, 1966, 1995.

Gurney, O.R. *The Hittites.* 2nd ed. Baltimore, MD: Penguin Books Ltd; 1952, 1954, 1961, 1962, 1964, 1966.

Imel, M.A. and D.M. *Goddesses in World Mythology.* Santa Barbara, CA: ABC CLIO, Inc.; 1993.

James, G. G. M. *Stolen Legacy.* First published New York, NY: Philosophical Library; 1954; New York, NY: The African Publication Society; 1980.

Lang, J. *Dictionary of the Liturgy.* New York, NY: Catholic Book Publishing Company; 1989.

Metzger, M. and Murphy, R. *The New Oxford Annotated Apocrypha.* New York, NY: Oxford University Press, Inc., 1965, 1977, 1991.

Morenz, S. *Egyptian Religion.* Keep AE, ed. First published as *Aegyptische Religion* Stuttgart, Germany: W Kohlhammer GmbH; 1960; Germany: Methuen and Co Ltd; 1973; English version Ithaca, NY: Cornell University Press; 1990, 1992, 1994.

Padovano, A. Mahwah, NJ: Ramapo College of New Jersey; 1995. Lecture.

Quirke, S. and Spencer, J., eds. *The British Museum Book of Ancient Egypt.* First published Frome, Somerset, Great Britain: The Trustees of the British Museum by Butler & Tanner Ltd; 1992. New York, NY: Thames and Hudson; 1992, 1993.

Radhakrishnan, S., ed. *The Bhagavadgita.* First published in Great Britain by George Allen & Unwin Ltd; 1948; New Delhi, India: Harper Collins Publishers; 1993, 1996.

Royal Sovereign Slim-Line Reference Bible. King James Version. Korea: World Bible Publishers.

Spar, I. Mahwah, NJ: Ramapo College of New Jersey; 1994. Lecture.

Tang, Ai-sheng. *Stories From Chinese Mythology (I).* Mahwah, NJ: Ramapo College of New Jersey; 1995. Handout.

Vermes, G. *The Complete Dead Sea Scrolls in English.* New York, NY: Penguin Press; 1997.

i. Barnstone, ed, 8.
ii. Morenz 212-213, 156, 333-334.
iii. Graves 55.
iv. Ibid 61.
v. Morenz 91.
vi. Ibid, 88.
vii. Quoted in Morenz 88; Radhakrishnan's introduction, 35.
viii. Morenz 120.
ix. Morenz 7.
x. Lang 11.
xi. Graves 381.
xii. Quirke and Spencer 71.
xiii. Morenz 105, 307.
xiv. Aldred 94.
xv. Ibid, 128.
xvi. Morenz 255.
xvii. Morenz 195.
xviii. Morenz 19.

The numbering of references begins again in the chapter entitled The Origin of the Texts.

ENDNOTES

[i] Ibid.
[ii] Padovano 1995.
[iii] Morenz 17.
[iv] Compiled from translations found throughout the entire text in Morenz including endnotes. In most cases, I believe the following to be true based on analyses of the above; the indication " ' " has been translated as the letter a;   the letter y at the end of a word is frequently translated as the letter i; any verb that ends in the letter i is indicative of the tense; a noun reflecting "the act of" ends in the letter t;   the indefinite article an is translated as the letter s;   the addition of .f at the end of a word is the singular note of completion; the addition of .sn at the end of a word is the plural note of completion; the symbol most closely resembling the following (ζ) is here translated as the letter a; a letter t at the end of a noun signifies the feminine;   a letter w on the end is the equivalent of an s for the plural and may be pronounced as a letter u. Where possible correlations to the English language have occurred I have placed the word correlation. I am only working with the words translated in the Morenz text and the definitions given therein, and apologize for any tensual or textual problems resulting thereof. While my scope is limited to the aforementioned, the Egyptian language certainly is not. I have indicated where obvious correlations have occurred as with god names. I am using the phrasing given in Morenz in order to stay true to the original definition, and not with plagiaristic intent.
[v] Dead Sea Scrolls Rule of Blessings, Section V 24-27 as noted in Vermes.
[vi] *The Ancient Egyptian Book of the Dead;* Introduction, 11.
[vii] Morenz 143.
[viii] Morenz 107.
[ix] Dead Sea Scrolls Nahum Pesher 2:12a, 2:13; I 4-9; quoted in Cook 135.
[x] "He is punished who trespasses against the laws"; quoted in Morenz 127.
[xi] Instruction for Merikare in Morenz 128.
[xii] Matthew 6: 19-20; Romans 3:27.
[xiii] Introductory Hymn to Osiris in Faulkner 27.
[xiv] Revelation 21: 10-11, 15, 18-19.
[xv] The Pyramid Texts in Morenz 39.
[xvi] Matthew 5: 29-30.
[xvii] Introductory Hymn to Osiris in Faulkner 27.
[xviii] Introductory Hymn to the Sun-god Re, Ibid.
[xix] Genesis 3:1, 14; Revelation 12: 9.
[xx] Matthew 19: 24.
[xxi] The Setna Story in Morenz 210.
[xxii] John 14: 1-2.

[xxiii] Introductory Hymn to the Sun-god Re in Faulkner 27.
[xxiv] Introductory Hymn to Osiris, Ibid.
[xxv] Psalms 23: 1, 4.
[xxvi] Introductory Hymn to Osiris in Faulkner 27.
[xxvii] Jeremiah 1: 18-19.
[xxviii] Morenz 62.
[xxix] Genesis 28: 12; Morenz 32-33.
[xxx] Gurney 4.
[xxxi] Quirke and Spencer, eds., 223; James 11; Spar 1994.
[xxxii] James 176-177.
[xxxiii] Budge's commentary on *The Book of the Dead*, 59-61.
[xxxiv] Ibid.
[xxxv] *The Ancient Egyptian Book of the Dead* Spell 17,44.
[xxxvi] Ibid, 94.
[xxxvii] For Peniel, see Leviticus 11; for Hormah, Deuteronomy 15; for Cimah, Ramoth and Mazzaroth see Job; for Cesil, see Job 38:31; for Ariel, Isaiah 29:1; for Bohu and Tohu, see the Haggadah; for Adoil, see 2 Enoch Chapters 24B-68; for Nisan, Heled, Lailah and Esh, see the Haggadah Chapters 1-2. For Harpocrates see Graves. Imel text referenced here.
[xxxviii] Ibid. 59, 62.
[xxxix] Ibid. 59.
[xl] Budge 10.
[xli] *Nature* **408**, 321; "Ancient Egyptian chronology and the astronomical orientation of pyramids" by Kate Spence.
[xlii] *Nature* **408**, 297-98; November 2000; "Plotting the pyramids" by Owen Gingerich.
[xliii] Ibid., 321; "Ancient Egyptian chronology and the astronomical orientation of pyramids" by Kate Spence.
[xliv] *Nature* **408**, 297-98; November 2000; "Plotting the pyramids" by Owen Gingerich.
[xlv] Ibid.
[xlvi] Ibid, 10.
[xlvii] Revelation 4:, 5:8, 5:14, 11:16, and 19:4.
[xlviii] Budge 72-74.
[xlix] Morenz 33.
[l] Proverbs 1:20.
[li] Morenz 33.
[lii] *Stories from Chinese Mythology (I)* 72-74.
[liii] Metzger and Murphy 183.
[liv] Ibid. 184-5.
[lv] Apuleius' *Metamorphoses* as quoted in Graves 72-3.
[lvi] Revelation 12: 1-3, 7, 9.
[lvii] Morenz 38.
[lviii] Brier 54 and The Learning Channel documentary aired the evening of December 6, 2000.
[lix] Brier 55.
[lx] Ibid, 54-55.
[lxi] *The Ancient Egyptian Book of the Dead* Spell 78,78.
[lxii] The Odes of Solomon has been described as "a Syriac Jewish hymnbook, in Christian redaction, subjected to Gnostic interpolations" (in Barnstone xxi.) "The Gnostics thought themselves the true and uncorrupted Christians (xix).

The Gnostic theology and lexicon[s] reveal Jewish [and] Christian... parallels and exemplify... the syncretic nature of religious traditions.... Thus after Jesus Christ is crucified the Jews think him another man and go on seeking the messiah, the Christians proclaim the crucified Jesus both man and God, and the Gnostics take the Docetic view that Jesus was only a simulacrum on the cross," for God is always God, but the underlying principle is always the same (xx, xxii).

[lxiii] Aldred 202.
[lxiv] The Learning Channel documentary aired the evening of December 6, 2000.
[lxv] I Timothy 2:5.
[lxvi] Quote from Zahi Hawass, Director of the Giza Pyramids; from a broadcast of The Learning Channel documentary aired the evening of January 15, 2002.
[lxvii] Ibid, 46.
[lxviii] Ibid, 230.
[lxix] Ibid.
[lxx] The Learning Channel documentary aired the evening of January 15, 2002.
[lxxi] Ibid.
[lxxii] Gurney 31-32; Aldred 170.
[lxxiii] The Learning Channel Documentary aired the evening of January 15, 2002.
[lxxiv] Malachi 4:2.
[lxxv] Book on the Destruction of Apophis, Papyrus BM 10188, 26, 2; quoted in Morenz 25.
[lxxvi] Egyptian and Chinese theory; ibid, 178-179.
[lxxvii] Morenz 178.
[lxxviii] Ibid.
[lxxix] Ibid.
[lxxx] Ibid, 1: 3-5.
[lxxxi] Genesis 1: 6-8.
[lxxxii] Ibid, 1: 9.
[lxxxiii] *Stories from Chinese Mythology (I)* 25.
[lxxxiv] Genesis 2: 9.
[lxxxv] *Stories from Chinese Mythology (I)* 231.
[lxxxvi] Ibid, 19.
[lxxxvii] Genesis 1:27.
[lxxxviii] Ibid, 2: 19.
[lxxxix] Ibid, 2:16-17.
[xc] Ibid, 3: 8.
[xci] Brier 19-20.
[xcii] Leviticus 11:13-19 as quoted in Graves 53-4; Deuteronomy 14:12-18.
[xciii] Brier 95.
[xciv] Ibid, 143.
[xcv] Graves 142.
[xcvi] Aldred in *Akhenaten*, 61.
[xcvii] Morenz 2.
[xcviii] Morenz 103.
[xcix] Barnstone xix.
[c] Aldred 18.

[ci] Barnstone 11.
[cii] Genesis 1:2.
[ciii] James 1: 26-7.
[civ] Acts 26: 2-6.
[cv] Acts 14: 44.

ABOUT THE AUTHOR

Lisa Ann Bargeman graduated with honors, obtaining a Bachelor of Arts degree in Literature from Ramapo College of New Jersey in 1996, a school once considered for Ivy League status. There she edited and contributed to the Trillium magazine. She has remained in the publishing field, and currently aids in the production of scientific publications in her home state of New Jersey. Ms. Bargeman, who also has a son, John Jaye Bargeman II, continues to pursue Egyptology and academics as a consultant.